First published in 2008 by CDA Press.

First Edition

Kick Litter: Nine-Step Program For Recovering Litter Addicts
By Perre DiCarlo
Design by Chen Design Associates

ISBN 978-0-9746582-7-8

LCCN 2008908115
Library of Congress Cataloging-In-Publication Data Available

Chen Design Associates | CDA Press
649 Front Street, Third Floor
San Francisco, California 94111
415.896.5338 | www.chendesign.com

Creative direction by Joshua C. Chen. Art direction, design and typography
by Max Spector. Illustration by Max Spector and Jure Gavran. Design
inspiration and photography by Perre DiCarlo. Author photos by Frida Stein.
Likenesses of Moxie and Cooper are used in these pages with their kind
permission. Names may have been changed to protect the innocent.

Printed on 50% recycled fiber including 25% post-consumer. Plus .003%
catnip — seriously, we added it to the binding! Stock is FSC Certified, acid
free, oxygen bleached, elemental chlorine free.

By printing on recycled paper, this first edition saved 13 trees, 5,727
gallons of wastewater flow, and 9,550,623 BTU of energy. Additionally, 39
pounds of water borne waste were not created, 634 pounds of solid waste
were not generated, and 1,248 net greenhouse gases were prevented.

Printed in the United States

*Attention: Schools and Businesses*
Kick Litter is available at quantity discounts for educational, business or
promotional use. For information, please contact moxie@misslitter.com

NINE-STEP PROGRAM FOR RECOVERING LITTER ADDICTS

 By — Perre DiCarlo —

# KicK LiTTeR

CDA PRESS

Hello, my name is Moxie.

**I AM** a litter addict.

I'M **Cooper**.

i dIG **LITter**.

**QUITTING** *was hard for me.*

By **DIg**,
I meaN I WAS a
**REGULar user.**

*Litter gave my life meaning.*

*I only did it to* **UNWIND.**

# It's hard to hide a habit

**WITH** litter between your toes.

My dealer WAS My best frienD.

That's the **BIG GUY** who feeds us.

*I knew where to get my* **FIX**.
*The litter box was always*
*next to the bowl.*

...but THEN our
soURce DISAppeared.

*He means*

**OUR** litter box
went missing.

*They* **KNOW** *what I mean.*

You don't know fear

**UNTIL** your stash isn't where you left it.

You find yourself
crawling across
the floor,

*jonesing for
your next hit.*

HUMILIATING.

## STEP ①

PREPARE KITTIES BY SETTING LITTER BOX BESIDE TOILET. CHANGE TO A FLUSHABLE NON-SCENTED LITTER AND A SHALLOW, CERAMIC BAKING TRAY. MOVE AHEAD EACH STEP ONLY AFTER SEVERAL DAYS WITHOUT ACCIDENTS.

## STEP ②

SET LITTER BOX ON TOP OF A BENCH OR CINDER BLOCKS AT THE SAME HEIGHT AS THE TOILET. USE RUBBER CABINET LINING BELOW LITTER BOX TO PREVENT SLIPPING.

## STEP ③

ONCE KITTIES ARE COMFORTABLE JUMPING TO THE HEIGHT OF THE TOILET, SET LITTER BOX ATOP THE TOILET SEAT ITSELF. CONTINUE USING RUBBER GRIP TO STABILIZE.

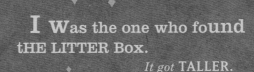

I Was the one who found tHE LITTER Box.
*It got* TALLER.

SEE FULL 9-STEP GUIDE IN THE BACK OF THIS BOOK

**WHEN** we jumped into it the litter box

*toppled over,*

so the big guy put some crazy rubber stuff under it.

*(mmmm, rubber stuff)*

You can't eat it!

I knoW THAt.

Now.

**STEP** 3 **DETAIL**

*RECOVERING ADDICT* - - - - - - - - - - - - - - - - - - -

*LITTER* - - - - - - - - - - - - - - - - - - - - - - - - - - -

*LITTER BOX* - - - - - - - - - - - - - - - - - - - - - - - -

*RUBBER STUFF (CABINET LINER)* - - - - -

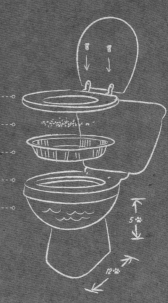

**STEP** 4

*SEAT* - - - - - - - - - - - - - - - - - - - - - - - - - - -

*LITTER (REDUCED)* - - - - - - - - - - - - - - - - - -

*ALUMINUM ROASTING PAN* - - - - - - - -

*TOILET* - - - - - - - - - - - - - - - - - - - - - - - - - -

*WATER (CONSULT PLUMBER)* - - - - - -

5

12

THE BIg guy
called the new
litter BOX

A

"roastiNG paṇ."

*He makes* **CHICKENS** *in it?*
*I don't see how.*

STEP **5**

POKE SMALL HOLE IN
ALUMINUM ROASTING PAN.

A HOLE!

STEP **6**

EXPAND HOLE OVER COMING
WEEKS WHILE REDUCING
LITTER TO A SPRINKLE.
KEEP PAN AND TOILET VERY
CLEAN WHILE KITTIES GET
USED TO THE WATER.

CAT FOOD

STEP **7**

ONCE THE HOLE REACHES
THE EDGE OF THE
ALUMINUM PAN,
ABANDON LITTER. LEAVE
THE PAN IN PLACE A FEW
DAYS TO COMFORT THEM.

8

water bowl

BIG HOLE!

ALUMINUM ROASTING PAN

LITTER (NOT PICTURED)

$H_2O$

No litter box!

We never saw our
old litter box again.

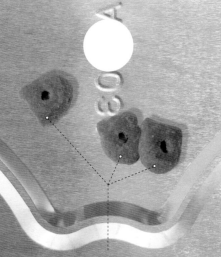

The next day...

(mmmm, chicken!)

**A HOLE**
appeared in the
aluminum.

It was the same
size as a morsel
of cat food.

ROASTED CHICKEN MORSELS
SHOWN ACTUAL SIZE

SERVING SUGGESTION ONLY

Aluminum is
NOISY

Every time
I hopped up,

the big guy came **RUNNING**
with a camera to watch.

*I like to
watch too!*

You kNOW...

thE FIRST THING you do when you see a hole is put your

HEAd in it.

*Hey, there's WATER in there.*

*4 or 5 paws deep!*

**FUNNY,** *it tastes better than drinking water.*

I can't beli**eve he's** makin**G ME DO** this.

# I hit rOck bottoM FAST AnD hard.

*Like any junkie, I found myself hunched over the toilet one morning staring into the reflection of a stranger.*

**I VOWED** *to turn my life around.*

*...once I finish this short nap.*

**TO** kick litter,
you have to find

*balance* in your life.

(girls learn faster of course)

I kicked litter in just 2 weeks.

We waited **2** months

for my recovery buddy to **KICK LITTER**.

I hid my BUSINESS
a few OTHER PLAces.

*The big guy always* **FOUND IT.**

i had A
little FALLING **out** WITH
the **wat**er.

Falling out?

You took a **NOSE-DIVE**.

*That looked like it hurt!*

EVERyone was
**disappoin**ted IN Me.

*I can be stubborn.*

THE DAY COOPER FINALLY
WENT CLEAN, WE CELEBRATED!

He **HOPPED UP,**

leapt across the seat...

and did   **HIS BUSINESS.**

ARrghh...

YEAH!

*A RECOVERING LITTER ADDICT WILL "SCRATCH" AROUND THE SEAT RIM IN A FUTILE EFFORT TO BURY THE EVIDENCE.*

*l miss litter.*

**MY** group says I'm brave to admit it.

I still dIG

LITter.

PEOPLE *don't know*
*what they're missing.*

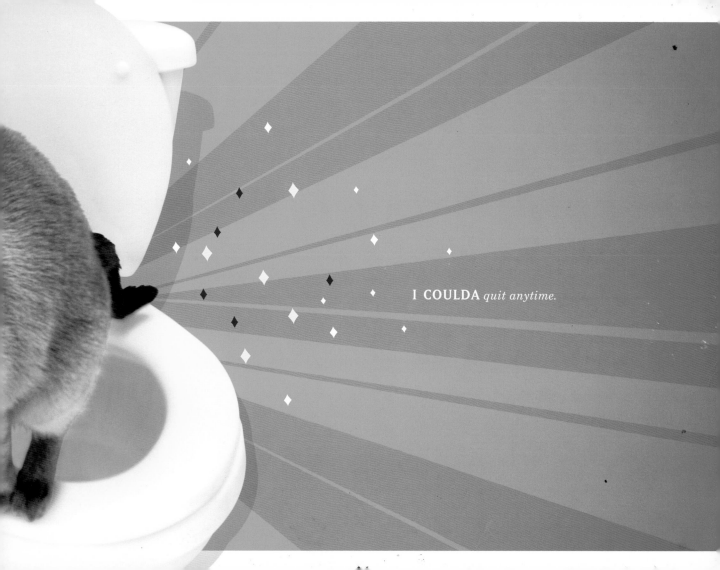

# KiCK LiTTER

STEPS TO 9 RECOVERY

## STEP 1

PREPARE KITTIES BY SETTING LITTER BOX BESIDE TOILET. CHANGE TO A FLUSHABLE NON-SCENTED LITTER AND A SHALLOW, CERAMIC BAKING TRAY. MOVE AHEAD EACH STEP ONLY AFTER SEVERAL DAYS WITHOUT ACCIDENTS.

## STEP 2

SET LITTER BOX ON TOP OF A BENCH OR CINDER BLOCKS AT THE SAME HEIGHT AS THE TOILET. USE RUBBER CABINET LINING BELOW LITTER BOX TO PREVENT SLIPPING.

## STEP 3

ONCE KITTIES ARE COMFORTABLE JUMPING TO THE HEIGHT OF THE TOILET, SET LITTER BOX ATOP THE TOILET SEAT ITSELF. CONTINUE USING RUBBER GRIP TO STABILIZE.

## SHOPPING LIST

- » FELINE
- » TOILET
- » LITTER - A FLUSHABLE, NON-SCENTED VARIETY, WHEAT-BASED IS FINE
- » LITTER BOX - SHALLOW CERAMIC BAKING TRAY (CERAMIC RESEMBLES TOILET)
- » BENCH OR CINDER BLOCKS THE SAME HEIGHT AS TOILET
  (DON'T USE PHONEBOOKS SINCE THEY DON'T HOLD UP TO ACCIDENTS)
- » ALUMINUM ROASTING PAN (HINT: THE CHICKEN-SIZE PAN FITS BEST UNDER THE SEAT)
- » TIME & PATIENCE

## STEP ③ DETAIL

RECOVERING ADDICT --------○

LITTER --------○

LITTER BOX --------○

RUBBER STUFF (CABINET LINER) --------○

## STEP ④

SEAT --------○

LITTER (REDUCED) --------○

ALUMINUM ROASTING PAN --------○

TOILET --------○

WATER (CONSULT PLUMBER) --------○

## STEP ⑤

POKE SMALL HOLE IN
ALUMINUM ROASTING PAN.

A HOLE!

## STEP ⑥

EXPAND HOLE OVER COMING WEEKS
WHILE REDUCING LITTER TO A
SPRINKLE. KEEP PAN AND TOILET
VERY CLEAN WHILE KITTIES GET
USED TO THE WATER.

CAT FOOD

## STEP ⑦

ONCE THE HOLE REACHES THE
EDGE OF THE ALUMINUM PAN,
ABANDON LITTER. LEAVE THE
PAN IN PLACE A FEW DAYS TO
COMFORT THEM.

8 🐾

WATER BOWL

BIG HOLE!

## STEP ⑧

CATS CAN TELL WHEN THEIR
PEOPLE ARE UNHAPPY WITH
THEM. IF THEY RELAPSE, EXPRESS
DISPLEASURE WITH A SHARP "NO"
(OR STAGE AN INTERVENTION).

## STEP ⑨

REWARD SUCCESS IMMEDIATELY
WITH PRAISE AND INDULGE
THEM WITH TUNA FLAKES,
AFFECTION AND PLAY.

misslitter.com diGlitter.com

TO LEARN MORE ABOUT THE PEOPLE AND FELINES WHO MADE
THIS LITTLE BOOK POSSIBLE, OR TO CHECK OUT THE PAPER TOY,
CALENDAR AND TRAINING KIT, VISIT KickLitter.com

**PERRE DiCARLO** is the award-winning motion designer behind the Harry Potter, Batman and Warner Bros. websites. A dog person by nature, he didn't know it was impossible to train his two new kittens until it was too late. He's currently completing his second book, a cautionary tale for celebrity kids: *Why Meghan (with an 'h') Shouldn't Bring Her Bodyguard To The Playground*.

**MOXIE AND COOPER** never wanted to be bowl models. They just fell into it. They blog about their misadventures online at DigLitter.com and MissLitter.com. Watch videos, download free stuff or stop by to leave a message.

The people at **CHEN DESIGN ASSOCIATES** are continually amazed at the opportunities that come their way. For example, they never in a million years expected to design a book cover with a cat sitting on a toilet seat. Other works by CDA may be found internationally and at www.chendesign.com.